TREASURES

OF A

CHILDLIKE HEART

MARY ANNE BRADY

eLectio Publishing
Little Elm, TX
www.eLectioPublishing.com

Treasures of a Childlike Heart
By Mary Anne Brady

Copyright 2015 by Mary Anne Brady
Cover Design by eLectio Publishing

ISBN-13: 978-1-63213-178-2

Published by eLectio Publishing, LLC
Little Elm, Texas
http://www.eLectioPublishing.com

Printed in the United States of America

Publisher's Note

For Mom, who gave me more than she ever realized.

And to the family and friends in these stories, thank you for making these memories possible.

CONTENTS

TREASURES

OF A

CHILDLIKE HEART

INTRODUCTION

I always wanted to write a book with my mom. Though we were forty-one years apart, our childhoods were very similar. We didn't grow up in the same location, nor did we have the same siblings, friends, schools, or material possessions. But in some time-transcending way, it is as if the same heart dwelled in both of us. A generation of time could not stop genetics, and a dose of something beyond our understanding created a lens through which we saw life in an almost identical way.

When I was twenty years old and she died, much too early in her vivacious life, that dream passed. But then I found, in a box of musty keepsakes, a journal she had written in college. It was like reading words I had written myself. Her thoughts and views on life were so similar to mine. Suddenly I better understood how I could honor her legacy: I simply had to live my life. I love the things she loved. The idealism she possessed I also have in great measure. The way she viewed her days on earth and her purpose for living were handed down to me. It was the miracle of motherhood.

I imagine her sitting with me now, speaking forgotten memories, allowing herself to get lost in a sentimental world—and me gladly going with her. To her, a memory was more than an occurrence in time; it was an event that shaped a life. If you will journey with me, you will glimpse some of those impacting moments in my life. Perhaps if you begin to identify with me in some small way, this book can serve to help you find joy in reflection and clarify your present motives. Not everyone's days of youth were as ideal as my own, but with the right attitude and childlike eyes of faith, there are always better days ahead.

May your heart be stirred as I share my own heart and some of the precious words my mom wrote down in her journal many years ago.

CHAPTER ONE

I didn't fully appreciate country living until I moved into the center of a metropolitan area of two million people. I began to desire, more than any urban convenience, those stereotypical notions of the countryside that I couldn't wait to get away from. Though I once breathed air that smelled of hay and plowed dirt, the city gave off only car fumes. I used to hear only calm stillness, interrupted every now and then by a cow looking for her calf, but then I had the inescapable drone of highway traffic. In earlier days, my panorama was gentle hills dotted with animals and oak trees, all basking under a sleepy afternoon sun. But years later, I saw mostly asphalt fanning out in all directions, buildings lined up one after another (as if it were a rule to cover up every square inch of grass and dirt), and cars anxiously speeding around, competing in a fabricated race in which no one wants to place last.

What I would have given for those smells, sounds, and sights once again. This memoir originated one day in college when I was especially frustrated with my surroundings. I had to accept that as much as I could wish for the way things used to be, I had entered a different season of life. And as everyone does, I possessed the invaluable but often unemployed ability to find the good things in every situation. So instead of complaining, I started to look forward with hope, while gleaning wisdom from what was behind, and opened my eyes to discover the blessings and adventure that were all around me.

> *The joy of simplicity. God made so many wonderful things for man to see, only they are not always right before his eyes. He must search them out. He must look twice to catch the little bug on a sidewalk or the glistening of dew on the grass just after sunrise, or the gentle sway of the tree as the wind caresses its slender branches.*

> *- Mom*

* * * * *

I was born in the Rogue Valley, in southern Oregon, and I could not have picked a more perfect street to grow up on. I lived on it for the first sixteen years of my life and never once ran out of amusements. Every time nature turned the page to a new season, a multitude of new discoveries awaited me.

The best thing about growing up in the country was that most of my entertainment was free. The flower beds became royal gardens for a princess of exquisite beauty and refinement, and the tall field grasses were the plains of Africa, where I tracked down rare beasts and birds. My imagination was the ever-flowing source of all my adventures.

Life was uncomplicated. At least it felt that way. My family usually only had "just enough," but I wouldn't have traded that for anything, because the riches we possessed were far greater: love, contentment, resourcefulness, and faith. My days as a child were not chapters of a fairy tale. I had my share of heartbreak, disappointment, and much-deserved discipline. I learned what it meant to pull my weight in the family, even as the youngest of four children, but my parents also saw the need to let me be a child rather than try to grow me up into a miniature adult before I was ready to blossom.

The theme of my childhood was simplicity. The world throws chaos and complexity at its inhabitants, and kids learn soon enough that life isn't fair. My parents saw the need to teach us to value the most important things while we were still young and relatively carefree, so that one day when we realized life was difficult, we would be built on a strong foundation of principles and would not be swayed in the storms that would come.

* * * * *

No childhood is complete without trees. If you have never climbed into the open arms of a tree and allowed it to envelop you in its green jungle, nor studied the puzzle-like pattern of tree bark and smelled its earthy goodness, nor held up a leaf to the sun to observe the hundreds of interconnected veins, you cannot understand how much joy a tree can bring to a child. It is the center of many games, becoming the safe base for tag, serving as a goal post for soccer, or transforming its branches into a mighty fortress for kings and queens and noble esquires. Trees are planted not simply to bring definition to a landscape but to bring life to a yard.

The ones in my yard were like good friends to me. The willow tree was of special importance to me. I can still hear its delicate leaves swaying in the wind, forming a gentle sort of wind chime. I learned every curve and branch and found perches on every limb imaginable. Somehow its very presence gave me a peace I can still feel, though many years have gone by. I used to sit on one of the sturdy offshoots while another branch cradled my back and yet another provided a comfortable footrest. I sat up there eating frozen blueberries on lazy August days, spying on the deer that wandered through our field or listening to the clucking of the neighbor's hens.

In a few instances, however, the grand old willow put me in a predicament. The first was due to a wonderfully cautious, discerning mother who wanted to avoid or prevent all worst-case scenarios. So she ingrained me with safety measures, training me to avoid kidnapping, drowning, or other nightmarish events. One afternoon, as I was sitting in the willow tree with a friend, we noticed a car driving past the house at probably twenty miles under the country-road speed limit. Granted, the road was at least a hundred feet away, but our young, nervous minds concluded that the driver had seen us and wanted to kidnap us. When we saw the car turn around on a side street and drive back, pulling into our driveway, we were paralyzed with panic. What could we do? We were doomed, and we froze in fear. The car door opened, and much to the relief of our adrenaline, I saw one of my brother's friends get out. He didn't even see us—and certainly had no thought of taking us—and walked straight into the house. We were more than a little embarrassed, but Mom would have been proud of our caution and preparedness.

And then there was one particular day in early fall (I was perhaps ten years old) when I decided to go sit in the willow for a few last enjoyable minutes before the evening chill and darkness fell. Unfortunately, shortly after I initiated that plan, my other brother's friends came over and started kicking a soccer ball around—right beside my tree. This would have been less of a predicament if I had not been in my rabbit-and-flower-patterned pajamas, ready to go straight to bed upon returning to the house. As it was, my mind was racing as I thought, "Oh no, cute boys are here and I'm in my dorky pajamas!"

Only one obstacle stood between the house and me: the boys. There was no way around them. I could wait it out in the tree, holding my breath every time one of them ran under it to get the ball and hoping Mom wouldn't come out and yell my name for bedtime before the crew left. No, that wouldn't work. My only other option was to make a beeline for the house. I mustered all the courage I had and hit the ground running. So far, so good. I was pretty fast. And then, to my horror, my brother started laughing at me. Then all his friends joined him, and I knew I could never again show my face to them. What a tragedy, and what a complication, since I knew they would be over at the house quite often. Fortunately, my emotions recovered from that event, and I still enjoy sitting in trees. But never while wearing pajamas.

> *Life, do you not wait for anyone? Yesterday I was but a girl. Today I am a woman, so they say. Not really—I still climb trees. Wouldn't they be scandalized? Aha! Bet they wish they could.*
>
> *- Mom*

CHAPTER TWO

My parents sometimes had large groups from our church over to the house for meetings or just food and fun. Once the adults settled into their business, we kids had a grand old time ransacking the toy drawers or running free on my family's two acres of land. We usually ended up in a boys-against-girls competition, and one particular fall day I remember playing a game I'll refer to as "The Last Leaf." Not surprisingly, it involved the sole remaining leaf on a towering hybrid poplar (that reached much higher into the sky than our two-story home). This leaf could not have been perched more perfectly if we could have planned it. It literally grew out of the very top of the tree trunk, encircled by the rest of the limbs, holding out their bare arms as if to say, "I'll catch you if you fall!"

Somehow we got the notion to try to make this leaf come down to us. One would imagine that a leaf that has held on that long, through wind and rain and loss of every other leaf friend it ever had, would give an equally strong fight against a bunch of hyper, reckless kids trying to get possession of it. But, in an unbelievable feat of shaking the tree (though I'm not sure how much our "shaking" really had to do with it since our feeble muscles against a tree trunk as thick as our bodies was not a fair match), the lone leaf began fluttering down to us. The journey from fifty feet high down to where we stood seemed to take an hour. The world went into slow motion. The girls' one goal in life became getting that leaf in their hands, and the boys were equally driven to keep the prized possession away from the girls.

I can't remember who got the leaf first, who had it last, or how long the game lasted. What I am impressed with is that we kids were entertained for a whole evening with such a simple game. Not only did it involve our imaginations and require no monetary investment, but we didn't even realize what a workout we were getting by running around like maniacs over a single deciduous remnant. It beat parking our rear ends (and metabolisms) in front of a TV screen, and I'm sure our parents were grateful for how soundly we all slept that night.

Anybody who had a remotely outdoorsy childhood will readily agree that leaves and autumn and fun just go together. I never understood that the fun I had with leaf piles actually contributed to the health of the yard, but raking up fallen leaves allowed Dad's manicured lawn to stay healthy by exposing it to the oxygen it needed. The catch was that we couldn't leave the piles sitting there past that day. If we did, the result would eventually be a big brown spot where the grass was starved and smushed. So we would either bag the leaves that day—after we got our fun—or rake the pile onto a tarp so it could be easily transported. One of these tarp piles surely broke a record for largest leaf pile. Imagine about an acre of leaves from trees taller than most houses all being forced together into one slug-filled, twiggy "cushion" of decomposing matter that had an intoxicating dirty-sweet smell and was slimy to the touch. What more could a kid ask for?

Raking leaves is hard work, though. After a while, my back hurt from bending at an unnatural angle, and for fear of overdeveloping one side of my body's muscles, I frequently switched the red plastic rake's position in my arms. Resisting the temptation to dive in before the pile was complete required a copious amount of focus. I had to indulge every once in a while, thus scattering leaves all about when I landed in the middle of them. Then I had to redo what I had previously done and continue on with the rest of the leaves.

This chore was certainly one of the most enjoyable of the seasonal yard work. The air was refreshing. The fresh chill invigorated and awakened my senses to see beauty all around. I could smell the sweetness that the rain brought. It bathed away dust and spread a just-washed scent everywhere. Gold and rust leaves shone brighter in the remaining sparkling droplets. Squirrels and birds busily stored food and braced themselves for the cold that would be coming.

Our feline friends also found raking leaves entirely agreeable. They pounced on leaves that strayed from our neat pile, or they dove headfirst and disappeared. Only their tails remained in sight, swishing around like a mischievous garter snake. On one occasion, Maggie, our beautiful, sweet-natured calico cat, came out to watch and play, but little did she know how much more involved she was about to get. My brother and I got the bright idea of helping her experience leaf-pile jumping whether she wanted to or not. Before she could even let out a mew, he swooped her up off the ground and threw her up into the air. The frantic flailing of kitty limbs ensued, plus a blur of fur and utter feline panic. But, as cats have a reputation of doing, she landed on all four feet, unharmed except her pride and whatever glimmer of loyalty she had left. The landing was soft, as a pile of leaves is, but before we could snatch her up to send her on another flying adventure, she tore out of sight like a multicolored lightning bolt.

We didn't always endanger the family pets, but we at least gave them a chance to prove their nine lives. Another time, my brothers and I got the smart idea to put Buddy, our rather large feline, on the roof. His obesity alone probably started making him fall off, but stricken with sudden fear, he leaped for the nearest object he could find at a similar height. Unfortunately, this proved to be nothing more than a canvas umbrella over the patio table. With one great ripping sound, he landed and fell through at the same time. After shaking himself off and jumping off the table, he was just fine, but we were left to do damage control. The duct tape was a temporary fix, but we didn't go too long before telling Mom what we'd done. That was the last time we put a cat above arm's reach for quite a while.

* * * * *

Every morning I awaken to look out my bedroom window, smell the crisp, fresh, brisk air, and watch the golden leaves fluttering to the ground or clinging weakly for a few last minutes in the wind. How lovely autumn is.

- Mom

As the trees shed their summer vitality, I discovered more intriguing things. Delicate maple pods, called samaras, resembled the wings of butterflies and dropped in a beautiful whirl that captured my attention. I sent these paper-thin helicopters flying over and over and watched them gracefully float to the ground. The locust tree also began to shed its curly brown pods, which my siblings and I liked to peel apart to reveal the curious seeds inside.

When the leaves uncovered the skeletons of the oak trees, massive clumps of green mistletoe became visible. Despite the Christmas sentiment this plant evokes, it is a pesky fungus that sucks the life out of trees. When we were old enough, my parents rewarded my friends and me for every garbage bag we filled with mistletoe. Somehow we managed to climb the trees with scissors in hand and ladder underfoot, snip the notorious bundles, and then stuff them into their dark demise. Two acres of oak trees abounded with the weed; we must have collected enough to spread Christmas cheer to the whole town a few months early.

The acorns also made the plunge with the autumn leaves. As they scattered, the nuts separated from the tops that attached them to the trees, providing me with supplies for a perfect miniature tea set. Due to the natural size of acorns, my only tea party guests could have been squirrels, chickadees, and other such furry or feathery friends, but children do not have to wrestle with what is realistic in playtime. Imagination is all it takes to be whisked away to a world where dining with animals is commonplace.

I saw enough small critters to entertain and amaze me almost all day long. The birds, bursting with yellows and reds and spots and stripes, vocalized their pleasant, untroubled songs and hopped and fluttered around the bird feeders that hung just beyond our back porch. The hierarchy of species was occasionally interrupted by the resolve and courage of a small bird motivated to gather food for her family and stock her pantry for winter. Part of me was getting ready for winter, too, and bracing for the cold and rain that would force me inside for a few months, but not yet. There was still so much joy to be found in my own backyard.

CHAPTER THREE

I've experienced a phenomenon that sometimes occurs in the fall. Under the right conditions, being sick with a cold can be somewhat of a pleasant experience. If the day is chilly and blustery, with leaves haphazardly falling and piling in drifts; if the home one resides in is comfortable and cozy; if the sickness provides an excuse to skip school, then the sniffles are certainly not too bad.

It was nearly a sacred experience to me. For one, I got to be home alone with my mom, who cared for our home full-time while I was growing up. Even though she was busy cooking food for six hungry mouths, washing mountainous piles of laundry, and trying to mop away the evidence of four children and multiple cats, just feeling her presence in the next room was all the comfort I needed.

Secondly, I got to do things that just didn't happen any other day. I could cuddle under blankets in front of the TV and watch more than one episode of a show. When I got tired of that, which generally didn't take very long, I could curl up in the recliner that was reserved for Dad when he was home and read a good book. All I needed within reach was a box of tissues for my nose and a trash basket to dispose of the icky ones. I called for Mom if I needed anything, and she checked on me every hour or so (not that

I had moved very far) to bring more fluids or some cold medicine.

I felt a weight lift as the responsibilities of life—whatever those were at the age of eight or so—were put on hold for a day. All my energy was focused on taking care of myself and getting better. And though I was never babied when I was sick, I still felt like the honored member of the family, if only for the day. I could delay my chores, I could savor popsicles, and I was guaranteed a spot on the couch. (For the youngest child whose designated seat in a household of six people was usually the floor, that was a rare privilege.)

Even today, if I'm sick and the weather and mood is just right, I'm transported back to a special place in my memories. Once again I feel the back of my mother's hand checking my forehead for a temperature and prescribing a heavy dose of liquids, and it's not such a bad thing to be sick with a cold.

> *I believe I envy a small child because I am no longer one with a carefree spirit. I am a woman in body but not in soul.*
>
> *- Mom*

* * * * *

On some crisp autumn days, the rains fell hard, pounding the roof and splashing the windows, daring us to step out of our tightly sealed box of wood and glass. My friends and I were driven inside after school, commissioned by Mom to be creative and find something constructive to do. Her threat of putting us to work around the house if we complained about being bored echoed in our ears. The first thing we were told to do was finish our homework. I remember the predicament of wanting to have fun with my friends but knowing we couldn't play until our homework was finished. Could we somehow combine the two? That is where our creative genius (or maybe just madness) showed up.

One friend and I had a method for getting our reading assignments done that probably drove my parents crazy, but they couldn't protest our methods of staying motivated to do schoolwork. We picked out the most comfortable spots in the living room and settled in with our books in hand and a gold apple-shaped bell on the table. This bell was normally housed on a glass shelf in the china hutch that sat like a sentinel in the homey but elegant room. But for this occasion, it served the most important mission in the world. Our method was this: one of us rang the bell, and we both set to work reading our individual books silently in our heads. Then, when the other one felt it was time, she rang the bell abruptly again, and we began to read out loud, wherever on the page or sentence we had finished off. Then sudden silence fell when one of us shook the bell again. It sounded a little like this:

DING ding!

"With one—just then—swift kick—Annabelle—the soccer ball—saw the—flew high—mysterious—and out of sight—"

DING ding!

soft breathing *muffled giggles* *pages turning*

DING ding!

"She couldn't—Coach Stevens—believe her eyes—high-fived—"

I was all for employing this method in the classroom, but I would venture to say the thought of twenty-five fourth graders all speaking at once at the command of a bell would make my teacher shudder. Needless to say, this practice remained at home.

As my mom's adage went, "Work first, play later." When the thirsty ground was saturated with rain and we had finished our homework indoors, we often got the craft bug and set out to create our own fun with whatever was lying around the house. Sometimes we filled rubber balloons with flour to create a squishy, stretchy toy, and sometimes we put our sewing knowledge to practice and created beanbags. With scraps of colorful fabric and Mom's help to thread the needles, we stitched two circles together, leaving enough room for the dry beans to slide in once the fabric was turned inside out and right-side-up. Once we closed off the remaining opening, voila! We had a brand new toy and many games to follow.

Our favorite spot to use these homemade playthings was at the top of the stairs in a small hallway—really more of an oversized landing—with doors on all sides. We made sure every bedroom, closet, and bathroom door was shut, and then we were closed into our own little cave (except for the gaping staircase, but every cave has a pit, right?). We stood in corners opposite each other and tossed the beanbags back and forth. On very daring days, we tossed two at a time, chancing a collision in the middle and an immediate loss of our catching streak. Somehow this mindless game kept us entertained for hours. We made up senseless rules, such as having to rotate to a new doorway each time we made a catch, which must have made us look like a very slow clock winding its way around the hours and minutes as we played up there.

Another version of our beanbag toss was up and down the staircase. Sometimes we just threw it up and down, trying to perfect the exact length it took to get the beanbag into the other person's hands. Other times we set a box at the bottom landing and tried to toss the beanbag in from the top. Buddy the cat thought the box would make a terrific nap spot, so we usually quickly forgot the beanbags and turned our attention to him. He had no qualms about forfeiting a nap for loving hands that would pet and adore him.

I leave you with a parting warning concerning handmade beanbags: though they may seem indestructible, a combination of water and then hot sun produces one very smelly bag of half-baked beans. We found out, much to our chagrin, that there was no restoration of the beloved toy once it had passed this point. Also, during the creation process, sloppy stitches will result in the bag bursting open on a particularly hard toss. But these problems never stopped us. With energetic minds and youthful hands, we found new fabrics and colors and sizes and made more fun.

Boredom was a word that was foreign to us.

*   *   *   *   *

I always looked forward to Halloween, but not for the same reasons most kids do. We didn't celebrate goblins and ghouls in my family, but instead we observed a long-awaited family game night. No television, no phone calls, no work—just enjoying each other's company and having fun together. We staked out the kitchen table for our board games or card games, and I was inevitably given a "handicap" as the youngest player, to my dismay. I just wanted to be seen as equally skilled. I didn't care about winning, anyway. We had fun searching our brains for the correct words, exhausting our eyes flitting from card to card, and cramping our abdomens from alternately laughing and tensing in the heat of a game.

But the fun was just starting! Whenever we heard a knock on the door, we kids would jump out of our seats and run to the front door, excited to add another tally mark to our penciled-in door count of trick-or-treaters. Since we lived on a country road where there were ten times as many cows and horses than humans, our list stayed pretty small. But we found some sort of unending amusement in it, nonetheless. On particularly slow years, we skipped the board games for a while and stared out the windows, watching for signs of movement. We knew where the only kids in the neighborhood lived, so we knew where to look. Somehow this continued to be a fascinating tradition for us.

Occasionally, the knock on the door heralded not someone *asking* for treats but someone *giving* treats. Many years, a sweet aging man up the road brought us homemade caramel apples to gobble up, and we enjoyed every juicy, sticky morsel with many thanks.

I never felt I missed out on trick-or-treating since we always had at least three-quarters of the candy bags left over for ourselves. We made precious memories with each other on those chilly fall Halloween nights. Family was truly the most precious celebration of all.

*   *   *   *   *

*You know, I'm happiest when I'm not thinking
about myself!*

- Mom

Few people stick out in my memory quite like Darrell. My parents knew him from their former church in another state, and this man had special qualities that set him apart from the crowd. First of all, he was deaf, but that did not hamper his communication. His expressive eyes said more than words. A little notepad was his gateway to a conversation with seven-year-old me. His laughter and smiles filled the room with a special, sentimental joy that caused us all to reflect on the important things in life.

Darrell played nickel hockey with me and showed no mercy, despite my age. I liked that because I didn't want to be treated like a baby. This is how it was played: we had a small wooden "rink" with raised wooden edges (that weren't quite high enough to prevent the coin from ricocheting dangerously on particularly wild hits) and little "goals" cut out of the woodwork on the ends. I'm still not quite sure what the hockey sticks were made of; they were too covered up in electrical tape, but they worked. It was the cheap alternative to air hockey but was just as fun.

His second distinguishing quality was his spirit of overcoming in the face of adversity. I dare to think he considered deafness a privilege. He was a loyal, dependable, serving, caring man. He had such a twinkle in his eye and harmless mischief up his sleeves that I think nothing could have stopped him from enjoying life. I admired his desire to travel and experience other people and places. He had to fly quite a distance to reach our home, but it was all a wonderful adventure to him.

I still remember waving goodbye as my dad drove him to the airport for his next destination. He had taught me the sign for "I love you" with my hands, so I frantically waved my fingers with that message, smiling brightly to my newfound friend. We all quietly walked back inside the house and considered what a blessing this man's visit had been. He taught us a great lesson: no hurdle is so high that it cannot be walked around or crawled under. This man chose to blaze his own trail and had a joyful, fulfilling life as a result.

CHAPTER FOUR

School was out for two whole weeks. Thoughts tumbled over one another in my mind in excitement and glee. This meant long days spent reading a book by the woodstove. It meant pistachio thumbprint cookies and decadent fudge. All shapes and sizes of wrapped-up mysteries that sometimes rustled, sometimes jingled when shaken, all nestled on a soft tree skirt under a canopy of green needles. And Christmas break, with all the hope and prayers I could muster, would mean that enchanting white fluff that falls from the sky under the right conditions. Yes, the next two weeks would be pure bliss.

The times when my grandpa made the trek from Alaska to see us (five hours in a plane rather than five days in a car) were extra special. Grandpa visiting meant special privileges, unexpected treats, and an extra-happy mom to have her own dad around. He was the perfect balance of sense and fun, prudence and pampering. He was a man to whom I gave my respect and my best behavior, not because I feared him, but because I honored his wisdom and character even in my youth.

The special privileges I received could have been because my mom's mood was lighter with him around, or maybe they were due to Grandpa's coaxing her to let me get away with some little thing. I remember talking (crying) my way out of a nap when I was about three years old, though with good reason, I might add. Grandpa had rolled up his shirtsleeves, tied an apron around his neck, and set to making a hearty batch of his world-famous (to our family, at least) chili. There was nothing that tasted quite like it. I may never know everything he put in the pot to create that outstanding taste, but one ingredient I am quite sure of is onions. How is that different from most chili recipes, you may ask? These onions were burnt. I'm not talking about smooth golden-brown caramelized onions. The vegetable was sautéed black and crispy. I'm not sure how healthy that was, but the flavor it gave to the meal was unmatched.

On one of these monumental chili-making occasions, Grandpa got a little zealous with the onions. Before my nap, I remember him starting the cooking process. My sweet dreams were soon cut short by the piercing scream of the smoke alarm. When I ran, tumbled, or flew—maybe a combination of all three—down the stairs, frightened out of my mind, I could go no farther than the gate that was there to prevent my aimless rambles up and down the stairs on unsure toddler feet.

As I shrieked over the noise of the alarm, clinging tightly to the bars of the gate, I felt imprisoned and thought surely my family would run out of the house and forget their littlest member, leaving her to be swallowed by enormous, unforgiving flames. Fortunately, this misconception was quickly ended when my mom came and picked me up from my misery on the landing of the stairway. Between sobs that debilitated whatever speech I could utter in my frantic state, I managed to plead to stay downstairs and not be forced to finish my nap. I'm sure legitimate fear was behind the request, but I know in my determined way I was also thankful to have an excuse to escape my least favorite part of the day, naptime.

Not all days were quite that thrilling when Grandpa came to visit. But they were certainly out of the ordinary. I remember being allowed to drench my cereal with flavored coffee creamer instead of milk, only because Grandpa was around. We would then have a cereal race, in part because grandpas like to make fun games out of just about anything but also to trick me into eating at the pace of at least an inchworm instead of a slug.

Grandpa was my captive audience when I wanted to speak, but my family never understood how I could eat so slowly. Allow me to paint a picture to explain my side of the story. Six or more people gathered daily around the dinner table, all sharing with great urgency the details of their day. Being the youngest and possessing a quieter voice, I tried to sneak in a word between their cross-table-flying conversations. But no, I failed and resigned to putting another bite up to my lips. But then I heard a quarter of a second of silence and tried to seize the opportunity! In my excitement to speak, the food fell right off my fork. And the words fell out of my mouth onto deaf ears because another conversation had already begun.

A lot of food-shifting happened on my plate, but until all the dinner participants left the table and I was left alone, not a whole lot went in my mouth. Thus, through that process, I ate very slowly. One method I used on myself when I was really, really stuck at the table was a little role-play. The green peas were people and my stomach was an airplane. I was too nice to make them miss the flight that was to take them on vacation, so I had to get them in there somehow. There was only one way down, though it was a tough path.

What a difference I could see in my mom when she was spending time with her dad. Not that she didn't feel fulfilled as a mother, wife, queen of the home, and all the other wonderful things she was, but her dad brought a sense of completion to her heart. Her mom had been gone for years; she died long before I was born. So Grandpa was the bond that connected my mom to her life as a child — that small part of her spirit that didn't want to grow up. She loved being his little girl. In reality, she was caring more for his needs than he was hers, but that tends to happen as parents grow older. She was bound forever to the father who loved her so unconditionally.

Now I know that only nature and God and my family of yesterday as a child and of tomorrow as a mother and wife will ever bring true joy. Life is too short to waste it in greed and selfishness. I am sure now that as long as there is someone to love and please, I can live with complete happiness in my heart until the day I die.

- Mom

CHAPTER FIVE

Coming home to be with my family again was like a reunion after many years. How at home I felt. With my family, I can be myself always.

- Mom

Something about a woodstove evokes a strong sense of well-being. Maybe it's the peaceful crackling of the logs or the enticing glow of the flames that calms the spirit. Perhaps the warmth and the smell contribute to the mood. Whatever it is, it brought our family together on dark winter evenings. Five humans (my oldest brother had moved away to college) and several cats crowded in that corner of the room, captivated by the metal box and convinced that nothing in the world was quite as sweet as that moment.

Yet with the sweet I felt an unexplained sense of nostalgia on those precious winter nights. It was as if I were mentally transported years ahead and then looked back, longing for life to be as simple as the woodstove made it seem. Right there, surrounded by family and peace and love, everything was perfect, but even at that age, I knew it would not always be like that. I had to cherish every moment of it.

I wanted to always be surrounded by comforting and peaceful pleasures and people who love unconditionally. But with the rhythmic march of time, surroundings change, people enter and depart, and we are left wondering what happened to yesterday. But maybe we all need to realize that our inner attitude will have a greater effect than any outside circumstance ever can.

We overcomplicate life. How many people sacrifice time, health, mental stability, and relationships just to attain a certain status or possession? Perhaps what we need most is to take a step back regularly and evaluate our motives. Why are we doing what we're doing? Too often we strive harder, driven by unhappiness and a lack of fulfillment, and we miss the opportunity to let go and focus on what is truly meaningful.

I'm not one to spin tales about walking ten miles uphill both ways in a blizzard to school. I won't sit around and give doomsday predictions about how "kids these days" will never be able to succeed. But what I will speak out is what I have learned in my own life: simplicity is irreplaceable. It cannot be bought or imitated. It is determined not by money but by the heart and entire purpose of a person's life.

> *It seems that the older I grow, the glamorous life of wealth and prestige seems of less and less importance to me.*
>
> *- Mom*

What does money buy? Perhaps a house filled with luxurious and labor-saving amenities. Money can be a catalyst for great things when the hands that hold it are wise. But although money can help us in our daily lives, it will never provide us with life. Many (both children and adults) search for happiness in "toys" of all sizes that turn into clutter, or they try to gain some unattainable status in order to finally arrive. Yet nothing but an urge for bigger and better lies on the other end.

As a child, I didn't know what our financial status was. We were four kids and two adults living on one small income. If it were not for generous grandparents, we would not have had our comfortable home on two acres. I had no scruples about receiving hand-me-down clothing, nor did I complain about my toys often being handcrafted or battery-free. The fact that most of our fun was imagined up at home and implemented outdoors in nice weather never bothered me. We built, we pretended, we chased, we played. We used what we had to make "new" things. We shopped at garage sales and gave away what we didn't need anymore to families who would treasure our well-loved possessions.

Money itself is not bad, but it can never be expected to buy peace and contentment. Even without much money, I feel like I had the best childhood in the world. I would not trade the experiences and love for anything else.

* * * * *

One of my favorite winter memories is of a simple gesture of Christmas cheer my family enjoyed and, in doing so, shared with all the neighbors. It was not plates of homemade cookies or banana bread, though we shared those things too, but a lone blue spruce tree. We kept outdoor Christmas lights simple, sometimes just framing the front porch, but every year we wrapped large colored bulbs around this tree in our front yard. It was a sight that warmed the soul and welcomed us home every time we turned up the driveway.

But the placement of this tree was what made it truly special. When you turned off the main road onto our country road, our house was about a mile down. It was a straight shot except for a slight jut to the left just before our house. This curve made it so that anyone could see the lit tree in our yard from the very beginning of the street.

It stood there every night as we drove home, welcoming us with its wide, colorful grin that pierced through the fog, rain, or snow. It was our beacon of light, calling us home and telling the neighborhood, "All is well tonight."

> *Tomorrow is going to be a clear, brilliant, sunny day! The stars are twinkling in the almost cloudless sky, and the moon is creeping across the sky, trying to keep its distance from the clouds. This is his night for glory since only on occasion does he ever come out!*
>
> *- Mom*

There was something so peaceful about those cold winter nights. It got dark well before dinnertime, and we lingered a little longer around the table. Our discussions often led to consulting the dictionary, because when you are raised with one parent from the East Coast and the other from the West Coast, you never quite know how to say certain words, or you just use multiple pronunciations depending on your mood. We entered many lighthearted disagreements revolving around this, and someone always ran to get the hefty dictionary to settle the score. Whichever pronunciation was listed first in the word's entry won out, and the advocates of that pronunciation were given the honor of possessing the most proper English, if only for the evening.

* * * * *

Come with me briefly to a more recent time. Early in my college years, I flew to snowy Anchorage, Alaska, during Christmas break to be with my parents in the home they spent a few years in at the beginning of their retirement. While I enjoyed the company of my mom on a more adult level than I'd experienced before, we were still always looking for an adventure.

A drop in temperature never equated to a drop in morale for either of us, so we layered up with gloves, scarves, hats, and goose-down parkas and headed out the door one delightfully cold evening for an exploratory walk. Though my parents' house was in a development with many subdivisions, it was just a block or so from a nature preserve. The sense of wild intruded into the residential area; before the bears went into hibernation, a few had wandered onto the very streets we walked that night. With them safely tucked away in their winter beds, the only menace we faced was the awkwardly graceful moose.

I cannot deny that something in us was looking for a little excitement and a good story to tell, so we may have been ready to make any little thing a grand production. One can only imagine, then, the giddy thrill we felt when we heard a loud, telling snort-moan-groan sort of sound coming from behind us. With the breathless still that had fallen over the drowsy houses that evening, any small sound seemed to ricochet off snowdrifts and skid across the ice, making it hard to tell where it originated.

We stood up straight in our tracks, whispers barreling out of our mouths, trying to hide the eager smiles forming on our lips. This was it. This would be our chance to narrowly escape a momentous and tragic end and live to tell about it. The moose is right on our tail! Isn't it? Do you see it? Well, no, but . . . there! It made the noise again! Did you hear it? Our heads swept the landscape like owls, looking for the culprit who was prodding our exhilaration. We only spotted lazy wisps of chimney smoke bathed in yellow from aged streetlights. Two bundles of nerves and animation, we started plodding home. Our boots had already proven to be not much good on the slick, icy road, so our only option was sinking our way through three feet of snow on the shoulder.

After doing knee lifts for about a quarter mile and nearly losing our boots in the abyss of snow, we finally burst through the front door with blood rushing through our veins and broad grins smeared across our faces. We couldn't wait to recount the experience to anyone interested in listening to our story, though at the time my dad was the only one in the house, and he didn't have a choice. Eventually, we calmed down our childlike enthusiasm and settled at the kitchen table with steaming mugs of tea, but it was a night we would not quickly forget.

Not every time we stepped outside held such grand drama, but Mom was sure not to let everyday life sink into mundane routine. On another walk during this visit, we grabbed the sleds from the garage and went to find the perfect sledding hill (something we were ever on the lookout for). After circling the neighborhood, we stumbled onto what appeared to be a gravel mound deeply covered with a white winter comforter. We took turns trekking up and descending down, each time creating a better, smoother groove on which to slide down. The person at the bottom was the watchman for cars, should the sled overshoot the small wall of snow we built at the end.

While we were laughing and creating bruises in uncomfortable places, a young boy from the neighborhood passed us on his way to look for work shoveling driveways. Mom noticed him eyeing us curiously and immediately struck up a conversation. "Have you ever sledded before?"

"No, ma'am, we don't have any snow where I moved from."

"Here, give it a try!"

The way his face exploded in joy on his first-ever sled run was worth more than we could have asked for. We eagerly encouraged him to try again, and after a few slippery slides down the slope, he handed back the sled. Mom, in typical fashion, effortlessly inquired about his family, his life, and what he enjoyed doing, and in the most natural and simple way told him of her faith and the reason for such joy in her life. The boy left with a brighter smile and an experience he would never forget.

She had a knack for doing that. Everywhere we went, her eyes were drawn to the person in the restaurant or store who needed encouragement. She never let an opportunity slip into the archives as another what-if. Some say it's a gift, others say it's intentionality. I say she possessed a little of both. While not everyone is born with a magnetic personality, everyone can look for a hurting or confused person. Watching someone receive a timely word of

44

encouragement and truth that helps them face their difficulties is amazing, but it only happens when someone takes the time to notice and act.

> *Opening oneself to the awareness of others around*
> *is one of the greatest gifts on earth—being able to*
> *make someone happy.*
>
> *- Mom*

CHAPTER SIX

Christmas in our family was always joyous. We didn't have splits and dysfunctions to be reminded of in a season that is often hard for families, and though we had no relatives within a thousand miles, we enjoyed spending time with each other and with close friends from our small church family. Our home was transformed into a holiday haven. Warm reds and dark greens decorated shelves, banisters, and tables; aromatic spices wafted from the kitchen into the rest of the house; and glossy bows topped hand-wrapped boxes, dimly reflecting the colored lights in the boughs above.

The highlight of the month for us kids was the advent calendar, mostly because of the candy but also because it extended the celebration for a whole month. This hanging treasure was a cut above the store-bought calendars because it was a labor of love, laden with good memories. The body of it was fabric, trimmed with lace and ribbon, and had plastic pockets for the days leading up to Christmas Eve. A part of the Christmas story was written on a piece of cardstock in each pocket, distributed evenly throughout the twenty-four slots. Under the words, my sister had drawn a picture to illustrate that part of the story.

These cards remained with their backs to us in the pockets until, each morning, we flipped the day's number over to reveal another magnificent piece of art and bit of Scripture. However, being children, we tried to hide the fact that we were often more excited to fish out the piece of candy hidden for each of us behind the cards. Mom usually stocked the candy at the beginning of the month but waited until the last few days to put in the big pieces that stuck out and revealed themselves to tempted little eyes and hands.

We were a Christmas Eve family. While other children eagerly went to bed early that night to hasten the morning so they could unwrap presents, we were already gathered in the living room, reveling in the long-awaited moment. (Sometimes we even pleaded enough that our parents let us open stockings on the night of the twenty-third. Since we kids didn't believe in Santa Claus, this was never a conundrum.)

But before anyone could peel back a sliver of tape or tear any colored paper, all eyes turned to Dad. With a worn Bible in hand, he began reading the account of Jesus's birth in Luke chapter 2. My eyes wandered to the large picture windows gracing our living room wall, and as I looked out from the dimly lit room to the stark treetops, bloomless flower stalks, and quiet stillness outside, I wondered what it must have been like to look up from a quiet night like that one and see a bright star indicating the loveliest gift of all. At that moment, wrapped in our own thoughts as we listened to the comforting words of hope, our hearts were so thankful for the One who had brought life and light to a world drowning in darkness.

As soon as Dad's hands closed the pages and placed the beloved book on the coffee table, we went forward in excitement, still being sure our actions showed thankfulness. As the youngest child, I was commissioned to distribute gifts from their resting place under the tree. We took turns opening presents according to age, so each round ended with me. Our gift-opening process was a slow one, but we liked it that way. I think the resulting gratitude was deeper because we were deliberate and unhurried. The unwrapping of gifts wasn't over in the blink of an eye, and after each gift the recipient got up and gave the gift-giver a hug. It was our sweet method of doing things, and we went to bed that night without the mental immobilization of suspense.

When daylight did roll around, we were in no rush and simply gathered in the kitchen for a delicious Christmas morning breakfast. We ate Mom's highly anticipated cherry pastry shaped like a candy cane, our favorite coffeecake, a variety of breakfast meats, eggs, and coffee and orange juice to wash it all down. We reflected on a year full of God's blessings and provision, and even if the year had been a financial struggle, we kids never knew it. My parents were great stewards of the money we had, and they instilled those values in us. Our quality of life was immeasurably greater than the quantity of things we had.

Most people seem to experience a range of emotions after the presents are gone from under the tree and the month of December gets ready to close its door. Some experience the Christmas blues, which seems to me to be a perfectly natural release of adrenaline after something is built up to for so long. Some give Christmas cheer the boot and slam the door behind it, glad to be moving on to the routine of life again.

But even as a child, I knew that the world had gotten Christmas all wrong. Who told us we had to shop like mad for two months, add new boxes of decorative clutter to the garage every January, and send obligatory Christmas cards to every family who sends us one? These things are not all bad; they are traditions that can usher in joy and respite for people stuck in the mundane busyness of life. But every year that passed, I resolved to make Christmas the most meaningful time of the year then and in the future. We did change it up some years, cutting back on presents in order to give more to those in need or giving donations to a special charity in honor of someone rather than giving him or her another trinket that would collect dust.

All in all, I was ready to move on after Christmas each year, and my siblings and I just had to be imaginative to get through the next few months of mostly indoor playing. Of course, our new toys helped with that, but when we were tired of using those every day, we had to create other fun and games. Sometimes we invented silly contraptions made of levers and strings that crisscrossed the room and could open a door or turn on the light while we were still in bed.

Other times, my closest-in-age brother and I created an indoor goal to kick our small plush soccer ball into. This ball was practically an extension of our feet, and we kicked it all around the house and passed it back and forth with increasing accuracy and agility. But we let loose with full force only in one area of the house. We opened the coat closet's double doors and set to work making the entryway of the house damage-proof. This entailed removing every painting, vase, or other breakable item from anywhere the ball might possibly reach or ricochet toward (we learned from close encounters how far this damage-proofing needed to go). Then, with quite the unfair advantage on my older, bigger, and stronger brother's side, we took turns unleashing kicks into the closet goal. It successfully allowed us to relieve pent-up winter energy, but it usually ended with us wistfully wishing for sunny days when we could kick a real soccer ball on the soft grass outside.

As I was walking (and running) back to get something, there sitting on the limb of a tree still bare of leaves was a robin. For a bird so small his chirping sounded like that of many—or maybe it was sheer determination on his part to not let loneliness keep him quiet, because he just sang and sang—and his determination did overcome any sorrow I may have had. He was a gift of joy.

- Mom

* * * * *

When I was nine years old, I was chosen to be in the annual spelling bee. This honor, however much it stereotyped a child, was secretly coveted by even the coolest of kids. Many young people can play a sport decently, and some can make music with an instrument or their voice, but few can spell really well.

I had always been a quick learner, and something rose up inside me to give my ALL to succeed in the competition. When the long lists of potential words were handed out to us before Christmas so we could study during the school break, I took one look at the pages of fine print and words I didn't even know the meaning of, and I was fully committed to conquering it. That meant while my friends were going to the local amusement center, I'd be studying. While they were playing games and calling their friends, I'd be reciting words that no nine-year-old would ever use in conversation. Christmas break would be no break at all. I had determined to be disciplined in my spelling bee preparation, but I knew

I needed to involve creativity to keep my wandering mind focused on the task at hand.

I devised a system of studying and burning energy simultaneously (a nearly impossible feat, but I've proven that it can be done). The long staircase in our house was perfect for my plan. I went through every word on the list by spelling it out loud while walking up and down the stairs. I held the papers in my hand, took a look at the word, and then took a step for every letter.

C-step-R-step-O-step-C-step-O-step-D-step-I-step-L-step-E-step-CROCODILE-step.

In this fashion, I spent the whole two weeks putting my brain—and legs—to nonstop use and probably driving my siblings crazy. But when the big day came, I felt certain of the words and was itching to spell my heart out.

We gathered in a large meeting room, waiting to be divided up by grade levels and assigned to our different rooms. There was a general buzz in the air: excitement mixed with nerves, tossed together with the hope of seeing someone you knew from a different school and automatically gaining a higher degree of coolness with your friends. The fact that it was happening on a school day added to the excitement, and participants of the spelling bee were excused from regular classes. I was thrilled since I, a rule-following student, was skipping class, even though it was "legal."

When we got to the room for the fourth-grade contestants, the suspense was brutal. We sat in our assigned seats, aware of the eyes of many eager parents boring holes in the backs of our heads. Round by round the chairs got emptier as students forgot silent letters or mixed up the order of *i* and *e*, and with sniffles and humiliation, ran into the arms of a waiting loved one for comfort. Suddenly there were only two contestants left, and one was me. I vaguely remember the congratulations and the ceremony that followed, but I cannot even recall the winning word. What I clearly remember is the trophy I was given: a tacky gold plastic bee mounted on a stand. But boy, was I proud of the achievement.

I cannot say that after winning I had a newfound passion and gave up sports and social life to delve into the mysteries of spelling in the English language. Instead, I realized that once was enough. I had my time to shine, and no competition was ever worth spending another Christmas vacation studying for it. I proved that logic the following year: I was selected to participate in the bee again but was eliminated within the first couple rounds. Inward relief overshadowed disappointment. This way I didn't have to live up to the pressure of a superhuman reputation. I could go on living a normal life as a kid who just happened to have a knack for spelling.

Honoring a child's achievements is like giving him or her a ticket to future successes in life. It raises self-confidence and promotes discipline and dedication. Unfortunately, some adults take this concept to an extreme when they affirm a total lack of natural talent or effort. If a child cannot sing, he should not be encouraged to become a singer. Maybe a student excels in math, but her parents prefer she play basketball and consequently push her away from her natural abilities and desires.

How smoothly our society would function if people were promoted and encouraged based on the effort they put into what they are naturally good at! However, many look past the fact that we are unique individuals and have a range of strengths and weaknesses. Instead of trying to equalize (essentially punish) smart, athletic, and publically talented kids to make those talented in unsung ways look better, maybe we should focus on helping all children find what they are naturally good at. With motivation and a little encouragement, everyone can bring something unique to the table and can contribute to a world that is varied in skill and achievement. Cookie-cutter kids do not grow up to be the kind of resourceful adults that make society function.

*   *   *   *   *

That same year, my parents allowed me to buy two rather unique pets, as long as I took complete care of them myself. When I had friends over during the quiet winter months, we often played with these dearly loved pets. These animals disgusted most people older than me, but they delighted my young friends and me. To their credit, according to the pet store, they were "fancy rats," which meant they would never grow as large or fat as their sewer-dwelling cousins. They also were adorned with much prettier colors, but their long scaly tails were still hard to fall in love with. Nevertheless, they were my loyal, sweet pets, Annie and Little Rascal.

Annie was cream and brown and the larger of the two. A cream spot graced the very top of her head, and her good nature was clear as she climbed onto my hand and up my arm, perching herself on my shoulder to observe what I was doing. Little Rascal, all white with red eyes in the right lighting, was more daring and adventurous, curiously exploring where she knew she shouldn't go. She wasn't content to sit on my shoulder; she preferred to rummage around behind my hair, trying to find a way to slide down my back and hop onto a piece of furniture that looked more interesting.

One school day, a friend came home with me to play for a while. We set to work making a fort for our companions, creating two compartments in an old box and putting a toilet-paper-roll tunnel between. We added bits of fabric and store-bought rodent bedding, but even with all our provisions, they seemed to have no interest in our creation. So we moved on to a new game—one that involved their participation, whether they liked it or not.

They became our characters, and our imaginations created the plotline. Annie was Bat-Rat and Little Rascal acted as Robin. They obliged to our holding and positioning them, but what ended the game was Annie's accidental flight across the room. Accidental on my part—the poor creature had nothing to do with it. I was whooshing her through the air, safely in my hand, when she suddenly just slipped out and went sailing on her own. We gasped in panic as we helplessly watched, and a small thud ended her flight. She slid down the wall, and I ran and picked her up, having no idea what injuries to be looking for. How would I know if I had given her a concussion or jarred her brain loose? All I could do was hold her close and speak apologies and reassuring words to her.

She turned out all right. She was sweet as ever and didn't seem to show signs of rodent brain damage, but I was much more careful with her from then on. She was not the first or last animal accident in our house. Around that same time, our new kitten decided to indulge his curiosity in a candle we had burning on our kitchen counter. Before we could swoop him out of the way of danger, he went over to sniff the flame and hastily retreated backward, rubbing his face with soft paws. When we got him to calm down, we discovered he had singed his whiskers and long eyelashes, and only a few curled stubs remained. The poor thing must have gotten temporary blindness in one eye, because he lost balance when he tried to walk and nearly ran into things several times. Fortunately, he recovered just fine and went on to be one of our most entertaining and loveable pets.

CHAPTER SEVEN

When I can find nothing especially meaningful that happened during the day, I can always look to nature—there always is a spot of enjoyment and perfection. Even in the changes of the sky or temperature, the land is intriguing at all times.

But haven't I forgotten something very important?? The most important thing to anyone: that of thanking God for this day—for my life—and being able to waken to the chirping of birds, to feel the cool breeze of morning touch my skin, to see the blue or cloudy sky. Oh, so many things to be thankful for and I forgot! How easy it is to take life for granted.

- Mom

The world was beginning to thaw. Soon light pastels would burst out of their bud cocoons and grass would shed frosty crystals and take on a slippery dew blanket. The air was turning from a biting cold to a fresh, sweeter breeze. The sky even seemed more radiant blue, and parts of my mind began to awaken from their winter slumber.

While I was thinking of soon being able to run free in the yard again, climbing trees, picking flowers, observing the birds and wildlife, my dad was preparing for a busy season of maintaining the yard. One job that was assigned to me was removing all the fallen branches and sticks from the areas to be mowed. I looked forward to this kind of physical labor because it exercised my cooped-up muscles and renewed my mind. I have never shrunken back from getting dirt under my fingernails or grass stains on my work jeans.

One particular year, though, I was asked to do this chore and kept putting it off. Finally, in a shameful moment in which I realized my disobedience, my dad ordered me to do it right then, that morning, without waiting any longer. The morning was young, and the sun hadn't yet burned off the fog and chill of the night before. I put on a heavy coat and gloves but quickly found that I couldn't grasp the smaller sticks with the ease and speed I needed to complete the whole yard, so I had to resort to bare hands. But without that extra insulation my fingers became cold and numb. They stung as the branches scraped against them on their way into the big bag. The air seeped up my sleeves and back and seemed to accentuate the soreness my muscles would feel after a few hours of bending and straightening, bending and straightening.

As I worked my way slowly and methodically around the mighty oaks that had dropped many of their fingers and arms in the strong winter wind, I grimaced at my consequence for not obeying right away. It wasn't often that I disregarded a request from someone in authority over me, and it surely did not happen again anytime soon after that morning.

Not long after that incident my heart broke with the disappearance of a loved one: my beloved cat, Tigger. It was early spring, and I remember the desperation I felt after about forty-eight hours had gone by and my parents told me he wasn't coming back. He was a strong, independent, alpha cat, but he showed deep loyalty to us and never left for more than a day. I hopelessly worried about what kind of trouble he had gotten into. My mind saw visions of ruthless coyotes and flesh-hungry raccoons. I stood outside every morning in both the back and front of the house, wrapped in a blanket to stave off the chill, calling his name loudly in a pitifully sad little-girl voice. I repeated my cries throughout the day and once more before my parents locked up the doors at bedtime. In my mind, their locking of the doors displayed their disbelief of him ever returning, even though I knew a cat couldn't turn a doorknob.

My hope remained. I knew his strength, his fortitude. I had to believe, deep down, that he had a reason for being gone so long. My heart knew he was still there; he was just delayed from being reunited with us. I never gave up calling his name, expecting him to show up, casually meowing at the sliding glass door in the kitchen.

And that is exactly what he did fourteen days after he disappeared. Miraculously—or perhaps I didn't give enough credit to his feline survival skills—he came home. The back door flew open and I was on the floor, trying to cradle him in my arms while he purred and wriggled out, making the rounds to the rest of the family members seated at the dinner table. I could almost see a smile on his face, or maybe there was so much of my own smile that it just spilled over onto everything else.

We often speculated what could have kept him away so long. Most of our theories centered on an injury, whether by a poisonous spider or an animal bigger than him. But after examination, he seemed to sustain no injury, at least anymore. Whatever the reason, I knew he never wanted to leave us. He had found a home where he was loved, and as much as he thrived in the outdoor environment, he knew where he belonged.

Another similar incident was equally distressing several years later. My cat Kramer disappeared suddenly, like Tigger had. He always came running back at night when we called, but this time, there was no pitter-patter of paws on the deck, no streak of fur running in the moonlight across the lawn. I knew that he much preferred hunting birds and climbing trees to being stuck in the house, but he couldn't forget his home, with a warm bed and premade food (no hunting required) at night.

I brushed the first night off, thinking he'd just found a jackpot of field mice and was feasting through the night. But the next day, when he made no appearance, I began to feel dejected and deserted by my own cat. I knew he loved exploring, but did he not know what this did to my little heart?

This time, my parents were not so hopeless, but they didn't seem to care as much as I did. He was my cat, and he really wasn't overtly loyal to the others. We had a special bond since the first day of his life. My parents had found his mother as a young, abandoned, pregnant cat on our country road, and in the warmth of our home, she gave birth to four kittens that very night. Out of the four, he was the only male and was often snubbed by the girls. But I immediately fell in love with him and gave him special attention. As he got older, he allowed me to put him under my bedcovers at night and slept there for a while before hopping out and curling up at my feet. I even made up a little bed for him in my doll crib, in which he gladly curled himself into a tight, furry ball and spent many afternoons snoozing.

He was my special cat, and it broke my heart that he'd gone missing. As in Tigger's case, I called every day for him and hoped and prayed that he was simply on an extra-long hunting excursion or maybe had found a band of friends to blaze some trails with in the uncharted hillsides. To my surprise, he nonchalantly strolled up the driveway one evening as I was playing outside nine days after his disappearance. He was calm and cool, acting as if he'd just stepped out to use nature's bathroom. I hardly stopped playing with and petting that little stinker the rest of the night.

A few years after our happy reunion, I was visiting an elderly lady down the road from us, and she was showing me some photo albums. In it were pictures of a stray cat that she said showed up on her doorstep every day for about nine days . . . and I could hardly believe my eyes when I saw Kramer in those pictures. I stifled my laughter and listened to her story, smiling and nodding, interjecting, "Ah, how sweet," and "How nice of you." But as fast as my feet could carry me home, I was all smiles as I told Mom what a little deceiver my beloved, mischievous Kramer was. And here I was worried that he would come home malnourished and haggard, but really, he was gorging himself on cat food that was likely more expensive and gourmet than what we fed him. It's a good thing he knew whose heart he truly belonged to and he didn't stay away from me for too long.

*   *   *   *   *

He said he still felt like a kid 'cause he and other guys went out and frolicked around, climbing trees. We talked about the struggle of growing up to adulthood from childhood. I said I didn't want to sometimes because so many adults were so serious

and never did crazy things. He said that he hoped I
never forgot my idealistic dreams. Always stay the
way you are—climb trees, lay in the grass, look at
bugs, watch the trees—never give them up!

- Mom

I try to remember exactly how it felt as a child to step outside to play and leave all my worries behind the closed door. As soon as my bare feet hit the soft carpet of grass, my heart leaped and spun just as my body suddenly did. I pranced from tree to tree, letting the rough trunks slip past my hands, peering at the sun framed by baby green leaves, and pulling myself up into the awaiting arms above my head.

I could climb the hand-fashioned wooden ladder into the platform high in the oak tree and see the world as a bird sees it. Nothing bothered me up there. I was a beautiful maiden in her tower chamber. Using a pulley system, I lowered a special silver tray (or wooden bucket, with less imagination) to my servants, on which special messages and deliveries were given to me. What is this? I am being summoned to a celebratory feast held by the royal family the next kingdom over? No, I must decline due to my previous engagement with a visiting duchess I am having dinner with. Yes, my life was filled with wonderful experiences and privileges, if only in my mind and in the books I read and stories I wrote.

When I climbed down from my post, I set out to explore the arboretum and botanical garden in which I dwelled—also known as my yard. The tulips held their pretty little heads high like china teacups in shades of velvety purple, red, and yellow, with splashes and streaks of other colors extending from the center. Their long leaves stretched like fingers from the ground, delicately brushing the petals and swaying slightly in the wind. Next door were the ever-optimistic gerbera daisies, flashing white-toothed grins and playfully dancing with the birds that splashed in the weathered grey stone birdbath.

I flitted from bush to tree to bush, spying dainty leaves with budding white flowers, feeling the thick deep-green leaves and stems of the rhododendrons and running my fingers over the stiff spines of the spruce branches. The heady scent of the daylilies carried on the breeze to my nose before I sunk my face into the lavender stalks and inhaled the calming fragrance. I gently stroked a few clusters to release the perfume onto my hands.

The life around me was invigorating, appealing to my sense of beauty and the need to run free and breathe deeply of a life lived richly in God's beautiful creation.

CHAPTER EIGHT

The wind blew in gusty wisps, rearranging all the fallen blossoms. What a free feeling the wind releases to those who notice. Nature is sweeping all troubles and problems into a little pile and shoving it under the doorstop. How clean everything looks and feels!

- Mom

The phrase "Let's go for a walk" can still evoke in me more joy than a kid feels when the first wobbly tooth comes out. My family often journeyed a mile or so down the road from our house to wake up our senses in the morning, or refresh ourselves in the lagging afternoon, or take an easy stroll as the evening light extended into later hours. This kind of exercise not only provided a boost to the metabolism but seemed to increase concentration and efficiency for the rest of the day's tasks.

As a child, I learned the details of every driveway, house, fence, and telephone pole. Anything that was within reach of my little feet or eyes was imprinted on my brain as a very part of my identity. I watched with fascination the little ditch that ran parallel to the pavement as the swirling eddies caught the yellowish foam in the center, and I raced twigs or feathers or whatever I could find in the quick-moving water.

I often hopped across and balanced on the thin strip of bank between the fence and ditch while my parents warily watched and warned of rattlesnakes seeking shelter in the very piles of rocks I was stepping over.

The neighbors knew us, and we knew all of them. I loved to look at their houses, yards, and animals to imagine what life for each family was like. The first house we'd see on our walk was a modest but well-kept home placed back in the trees; the familiar Jeep was parked outside and the ever-present barn cat was hunting small creatures. Further down, we passed the small house with the driveway that led over the bridge and around the bend. I walked by on tiptoe with wide eyes, knowing the resident dogs were not fond of strangers on or nearby their land.

Then there was the doctor and his family with the all-American house set back in the midst of lush green fields. The wraparound porch framed white siding and bright shutters, and the irrigation sprinklers sang a peaceful, rhythmic melody as a doe and her fawns cautiously grazed in the sections yet untouched by the water. On the other side of the road, an elegant brick-framed gate revealed a long, treelined driveway that seemed to end with a big red front door standing out in the middle of a classic colonial-style house. I always tried to imagine what the inside of that beautiful home, with its balconies and paned windows, looked like.

Many barns of various styles and ages dotted the landscape, some boasting new paint and some hunched over a bit on their foundations, weighed down by years of sheltering animals and equipment from the elements. Skittish horses shyly skipped away as our steps drew near, and curious cows stared, expressionless, as I loudly mooed at them. Occasionally, as the days got warmer, a long garter snake slithered onto the pavement to warm his belly.

At the end of the main road was the prize, the shining jewel of the walk. Though it appeared to be just a muddy pond surrounded by weeds and duck droppings, it offered far more joy and amusement to the truly appreciative visitor. There were bunches of quiet, unassuming ducks with which we shared our leftover bread heels. It always made me laugh to see them squabble and squawk for the crumbs and then go right back to their simple floating life. If we were fortunate, we might see the turtles sunning themselves on logs that jutted out of gently rippling water. If I grabbed hold of one of the sturdy tree trunks and leaned over, I sometimes caught a glimpse of a darting catfish. Trees clustered in leafy groups around the small reservoir, some producing mysterious fruit that we dared each other to taste and then spit out because it was so sour. Just past the pond, the road turned into a one-lane dirt road that wound up the hillside next to a bubbling creek and afforded a magnificent view of the serene valley stretched out below.

I never wanted our walks to end, but I knew we could always go again. And when we did walk again, I seemed to discover completely new things, but maybe that was only because I had eyes to search for the details others might not even notice. This land I loved never grew old to me.

> *There's so much to see and do if a person only would quiet down and look around.*
>
> *- Mom*

* * * * *

How does a butterfly know when to emerge out of its cramped cocoon, and who teaches it to fly when all it has ever known is walking on little legs? When did the sunflower realize it could pivot its oversized head on a skinny neck to follow the warmth of the sun? And really, who teaches that new puppy to be so loyal, energetic, and lovable? It seems when a person wants to find inspiration, they look to a faraway place or a children's storybook laden with creative imagination. Wouldn't it be even more special to put on watchful eyes and observe the everyday wonders around us, objects whose natural response in life is to praise their Creator?

I once noticed the unwavering courage of a small bird defending its babies from larger predators. It was a feat worth great recognition, but to the bird it was simply instinct. Another bird portrayed the self-sacrifice of a loving parent by risking its life to fly out into a hailstorm to draw a threatening human away from the nest.

A third example I always found amazing was that of the killdeer. They are curious birds that lay their eggs right on the ground, on the shoulder of a road or in a rocky area, which seems to be the most unlikely and dangerous place for survival of such delicate objects. But the cunning plan of the killdeer is what keeps this species alive and well. When an approaching creature gets too close, one of the parents will begin to put on a dramatic display of injury, pathetically chirping while limping and holding out a wing, walking deliberately away from the nest. The hope is that whatever intention the invading creature has, whether foraging for food or otherwise, it will be diverted by this much easier target. The bird keeps a good pace, just enough to continue to draw the threat away. When it feels it is far enough from the nest, it suddenly, "miraculously" spreads its wing and lifts off the ground, flying back to the nest in a very roundabout way, just in case the threat is still watching.

I loved watching this smart ruse, and I always carefully observed the bird's return flight to the nest so I could mark the spot and come take a look later. Only experienced eyes could spot the eggs due to their amazing camouflage. Speckles blended with the grey and brown earth on which they sat, and their placement was just perfect among a few other rocks or raised objects.

The only reason these defenseless creatures survived was because someone else willingly loved and protected them. What a beautiful pattern for us to follow. The sacrifice learned from a simple bird could be the very thing that saves a life.

Nature is one of the Lord's perfect examples.

- Mom

* * * * *

Something unique happens when a person steps out of the comfort of boundaries and fences and into the wild unknown. The sense of feeling small, like one piece of an intricate and beautifully crafted puzzle, is important from time to time.

This morning I woke to the chirping of singing birds on their daily hunt for food. It was 5:30 in the morning and the sky was barely blue in color. I dressed quickly in jeans and sweatshirt and was out the door.

The first sight was from the steps where I sat watching and getting prepared—cleaning the dust and cobwebs from the hazy mind. Birds flew in all directions, chasing one another or searching for breakfast. Their favorite roosting ground must have been the young tree half covered with white blossoms that was directly in front of our steps across the street. The soft white blooms that had in previous days fallen gently to the floor of nature decorated the grass in snowy whiteness. Here the robins and swallows made their momentary rests.

As I continued on to where the virgin forest lay, a feeling of peace and serenity began to overcome my senses. It felt as though maybe my mind was opening up and was a temporary vigil for anything God might have to say to me. He did speak. Through the birds and trees and sky and flowers did he reveal his love — but how many times one forgets to listen. I had a difficult time trying to make a specific prayer out in those woods. I just wanted to blend in with nature and be part of it — and listen.

- Mom

My wild unknown as a child was down the road, up the hill, and beyond the gate to the irrigation ditch. Because we lived in county land, not within city limits, the only water we had was from our own well or holding tank rather than city water. Since everyone on and near our country road had at least an acre of land to maintain — most had many more —

the irrigation ditch was an essential part of life. By the time it trickled into our backyard, it was a slender stream that meandered under the watchful eyes of tall grasses and quaint wooden planks that served as bridges for us kids. But higher up on the hill, it flowed wider and deeper, rushing through a series of filters and grates, eager to flow into the fields and be put to good use.

The neighbors—a generally friendly bunch of country folks who shared with each other extra chicken eggs or vegetables and waved when passing on the road—rotated the job of cleaning the upper ditch and its filters seasonally, and my dad usually took one of us siblings with him when it was his turn. I will never forget the day I crossed over the line of safety into the realm of the bull for the first time. I had only heard stories of how large (very true) and ferocious (maybe partially true) he was. He might as well have been a super-powered beast in my youthful mind.

The moment I caught a glimpse of him resting under some wide-spreading oaks, my gaze was frozen. I couldn't force myself to look away from the very thing that could send me flying from the hillside to the bottom of the valley below, and yet everything in me said, "Look away! Don't let him make eye contact and you'll be alright!" I thought I saw smoke pour out of his nostrils—

"Come on, hon. The ditch is this way." Dad's voice brought reality back. "Now be careful where you step since this is cow pasture, and just be aware of the bull."

Aware? Oh, little did he know how aware I was.

Time went slowly for those twenty minutes. I felt sure we were going to receive due punishment for invading the mighty beast's home turf, but to my surprise, he just stayed under his trees and didn't bother even stomping a hoof in our direction.

The view from high up on the hillside was gorgeous. I saw many familiar landmarks in the valley below, and the rolling mountains standing guard on all sides of us made me feel protected. But the real sense of euphoria came when we walked back to the fence, clicked the gate behind us, and got into the car to start the descent back to our house. I could hardly believe it! I had survived the bull! I was brimming with excitement and felt just a little bit braver and stronger that day to face any other challenge. After all, I survived the wild unknown of the bull.

CHAPTER NINE

*It's almost SUMMER! Love that sun and sky and
wind—yippee!*

- Mom

As soon as the days started getting warmer and the
raindrops held back to rest in the comfort of the cushioned
clouds, we almost daily brought out of hibernation a box
way up on the top shelf of the coat closet. Pulling apart the
flaps of the box revealed cotton threads of sun-faded coral
and cream colors, beautifully woven into the most
comfortable, restful Mayan hammock. As my siblings and I
skip-walked to the designated trees—too much excitement
to waste any time—we could practically feel the rhythmic
swaying already and dreamed of spending many breaks
from our energetic play this way.

I got there first and grasped the familiar metal hook
protruding from one of the solid oak trees. Then our nimble
fingers got busy untangling and straightening the hammock
to position it in place on the two hooks that would suspend
it in perfect weightlessness. It only took one moment to
glance at our proud work before two of us scrambled into
the stretchy, swinging bed. For a moment we lay perfectly
still, stretched out like string beans side by side. This was a
special feeling. Our land-locked legs reveled in the chance to

be hanging, waving above the ground like stray feathers carried on the wind. The stillness only lasted a few seconds; soon one kid got kicked out so the other could stretch out perpendicular to the weave of the threads, asking for a good push from behind and looking up at the leafy branches waving down at the funny sight.

If I was the one back on land for the moment, I had to think of something entertaining to do, so I reached down and filled my fists with grass, waiting for the swinger's legs to reach higher than my head before tossing up a green shower that would fall as he or she swung back toward me. After I was scolded for that, I lay flat on my back, slightly to the side for fear of moving body parts crashing down on me, and timed little pokes or jabs just perfectly to surprise the one peacefully floating above me.

We soon switched places, and I wrapped the edges all around me so I looked like a peapod, peeking out between gaps to watch the world methodically rocking up and down. I was safe from everything—except tickling hands trying to get me at the right moment as I swung toward their impending doom. I felt like a little caterpillar, sure that the moment I crawled out from the tight wrap, I would be enabled to fly on my own with wings the hammock itself granted me.

Alas, it never happened, so we were forced to revisit the hammock day after day, always feeling for those minutes or hours that we really were free to soar above the limits of the earth—or at least dangle a few inches from it.

> *The dazzling beauty of our surroundings back in that valley of green, white, and blue was enough to not urge us to leave soon. How relaxing to lie on that mossy mountainside and gaze at the sky with its billowing, puffy white clouds.*
>
> *- Mom*

My brother and I must have really wanted to fly. Since the hammock always brought us back to earth after propelling us forward and backward, the old wooden swing could certainly give us the liftoff we were seeking. The swing itself, full of home-hewn character, looked like it could snap in half from any exuberant movement. Grandpa had lovingly crafted the wooden seat that was strung with a thick rope up either side for gripping support. Surplus strips of linoleum from our kitchen floor were wrapped between the rope and the big tree limb to prevent the bark from being stripped off. The branch this playtime masterpiece hung from was not excessively high off the ground, so the height the swing reached when we pumped our legs with all our might was not too far from the ground. Still, it was enough that we managed to launch off onto a blanket laid out below.

When we worked with momentum, we had the exhilaration of flying, if only for a moment.

This game was great fun until, once, I thought the swing tried to kill me. On a free-flying launch, I must not have thought quickly enough about my landing, because I landed firmly and abruptly on my behind, a motion my body was not prepared for. In a process I had never experienced before and could only describe as dying in my naiveté, I suddenly had no breath in my lungs and seemingly no capability to draw in oxygen. Really, I just got the wind knocked out of me, but I felt as if my soul had been sucked right out the top of me. While my brother stood by, either oblivious or unsure what to do, I eyed the distance between where I was now sprawled and the back door. Having no other option, I began the tortuous crawl on hands and knees to see my parents with my own eyes for the last time before my world went dark.

I pulled myself up one step, then another, then across the boards of the deck and dragged open the sliding glass door. Just as I hoped, my sister and dad were sitting in the kitchen, and with much drama, I managed to eek out, "I can't . . . breathe . . . I think I'm . . . dying . . ." The lack of sympathy I met with was not what I had hoped for. My sister showed no reserve in her laughter, and my dad, concealing his snickers much more appropriately, assured me calmly and gently that I was going to be just fine. And, sure enough, I already was starting to feel a bit more normal! My breath came back in measured cadence, and the soreness of my tailbone gradually wore off, as most injuries inflicted on young bodies seem to do.

Not all my activities could be deemed so dangerous (and certainly not for a while after that incident). I often dawdled away slow summer afternoons by sitting under the embracing arms of my favorite tree, the willow that proudly stood alone away from our house. From here I could observe the patterns of clover in the yard or listen to the neighbors' horses calling to one another or spy on intriguing neighbors and cars that passed the house. My best companion during these times was my valiant, handsome Tigger, who had been in the family since before I could remember. The breeders promised he was full-blooded Siamese when my parents bought him, but he seemed to have only a trace of the breed's facial features and no other indicators. His body was sturdy, all muscle and not an ounce of fat to be found or jiggled. His stripes accentuated his stride as he walked, and his gentle blue eyes seemed to smile in the sweetest way when he looked at those he loved.

Fiercely loyal to his people, he defended our two acres with the dignity and intensity of a mighty lion. I often saw him sitting on the very edge of our property, practically asking for a neighboring cat to cross the invisible line and see what would happen. But he wasn't always wild-natured.

In fact, as I sat under the swaying leaves of the willow and called for him to come, he trotted over with all the happiness in the world in his eyes, nuzzled into my outstretched hands, and settled down next to me to enjoy the beauty in every direction. He was my protector, my friend, my Tigger. I was so concerned about his well-being that when my parents told me one day they had to take him to the vet to get neutered—a concept I had very little knowledge of—I asked very seriously if he could still have girlfriends in the neighborhood after that took place. With smiling eyes, they assured me that yes, he certainly could.

> *How often do we take time out from a busy day to stop in our tracks to just sniff the fragrant air or pet a passing dog or catch the rustling of the leaves high in the trees? Let me never forget!*
>
> *- Mom*

* * * * *

My brother and I still say we are quite possibly one of the best brother-sister Frisbee teams in the world. We may not have much exposure to actual professionals and statistics, but we just know the many hours we spent throwing the disc back and forth, creating obstacles to dodge or setting goals to achieve for number of catches. All we had was an inexpensive plastic Frisbee (or occasionally a football or soccer ball to mix it up), but we made do and it worked just perfectly. Even our cat Maggie joined the fun. When we tossed the Frisbee anywhere in her area, she chased and pounced on it, then waited like a dog for us to throw it again. This odd cat also liked to play in the sprinklers, but only if no one was looking. I distinctly remember watching through a window as she looked around to check if any humans could see and then jumped right into the path of the spray. Springing out of the way once she was soaked, she quickly licked herself and then pounced right back into the same spot where she'd gotten drenched before.

We filled our days with simple amusements like these or sometimes more daring ones, such as testing the electric fence with a blade of grass and feeling the pulse up our hands and arms. Always, no matter what the activity was, our feet became stained green and brown, since we never wore shoes in the yard. This naturally resulted in stepping on bees or prickly thistle plants, but the feeling of the soft grass between our toes and the ground cooling our feet as we ran was worth those risks. I always tried to clean my feet well enough by wiping them on the welcome mat, but without fail, my mom checked the undersides and discovered that the stains needed to come off with scrubbing. Even a pleasant bunch of carefully arranged wildflowers—pink snapdragons, blue bachelor's button, and yellow poppies—would not convince her otherwise, so off to the tub I went to wash away the evidence of a long and fulfilling playtime outside.

CHAPTER TEN

Can't you feel what I am experiencing? Freedom of mind to grasp and partially digest all within reach—to explore all facets of life—to be uninhibited!

- Mom

There were so many natural wonders to discover in my own backyard—wonders of new life, imagination, and neighborly love. Summer was not a time to stop learning because classes were no longer in session and homework was not being assigned. No, on the contrary, I think summer was when we learned the most.

Every year we learned how to care for and respect new life. We were blessed to live in monarch-butterfly territory and to be able to see firsthand their incredible transformation from caterpillar to free, winged miracle. Just about every day, armed with "bug barns," we set out to the milkweed plants to see if the caterpillar eggs had been laid or had hatched yet. Once we found them alive and well and growing large and fat, we carefully picked one off the plant and put it into its newly prepared home, complete with branches for climbing amusement and milkweed leaves for continuing to grow plump. Day after day we watched it until, to our extreme delight, the moment came when the caterpillar hung upside down from the top of the container.

As more days passed, we watched the cocoon slowly transform from a soft layer of transparent silk to a hard shell.

Waiting for that caterpillar to emerge a new creature was like putting warm chocolate chip cookies and milk right under a hungry child's nose but telling them to wait a few hours. Even worse, this was days instead of hours. Every morning I ran down the stairs, through the kitchen, and out the back door to check on our cocoon. The thrill when I saw cracks forming in the hard shell was unlike any other experience. I sat and waited as long as I could—a great lesson in patience—but as Mom reminded me often, "A watched pot never boils." I checked back over and over, probably no more than five minutes apart, until Mom assigned me some chore that required undivided attention. Imagine my elation when orange and black came into sight and the jade-colored shell turned into a thin, papery skeleton of a former life!

The emerging monarch cautiously tested the enclosed world around it, lifting only one foot off the cocoon at a time, slowly spreading expansive, flame-colored wings and lifting up, down, up, down. The gentleness with which it tried out its new body was essential, and I once made the mistake of touching one too early and bearing the guilt of delaying her independence. Though in my childishness I injured it, I became her most devoted and gentle caretaker. This special creature I named Lefty, since it was her left wing that kept her from flying.

Every morning, afternoon, and evening was mealtime for her, and I opened the bug barn and positioned my finger at the opening. She accepted my extended invitation and we began feedings. I gently lifted her through the sweet-smelling air, allowing her to feel the breeze that she already should have been flying through. As we neared the potted plants on the porch, I lowered my finger so it was touching the center of a flower, and she hopped off to drink her fill of sweet nectar. As I watched her happily fill her belly, I was in awe of the transformation that had happened. One worm-like creature with an abundance of legs and a tendency toward gluttony had allowed herself, through hard work and patience, to be turned into what her purpose was all along—a picture of freedom, grace, and beauty.

Was there a lesson for me to learn through this example? Could I allow circumstances that were not always pleasant to shape me into something much greater if I only withstood the discomfort? While I still pondered those deep thoughts, Lefty took her place on my finger once again, and I was inspired to anticipate and accept change with open arms, for it often submitted me to a much greater plan than I was aware of.

I am happy to report that Lefty recovered full mobility of her wing, and after many cherished days of walks and feedings with her, I watched her soar into the sky to enjoy the independence she was always meant to have. As much as I didn't want to let her go, I knew that would be like keeping her a caterpillar forever. It would be a form of life but without all the blessings and liberty intended. How true for some humans who refuse to be shaped through difficulty into something more amazing than they ever imagined possible.

* * * * *

It would have been easy for adult eyes to miss, but a clubhouse straddled the property line between the neighbor girls and us. Enclosed by oak trees on three sides, we didn't have much to build except a modest bridge spanning the small ditch that ran through the middle. We had covered-hole traps and a lookout limb to spot intruders coming from any direction across the wide fields surrounding us. We made a hand-washing station out of a milk jug with a drilled hole and a pencil to stop up the flow, and we hung up a pair of old nylon stockings filled at the bottom with soap scraps. (Having clean hands while playing outside was never the point, but being able to boast about having a clubhouse with a sanitation station probably was.)

One fort was not enough, however, and we set out to build the classic tree fort to provide variety in our meeting place and activities. With a sturdy oak picked for the purpose, we nailed the boards and planks across the Y in the trunk. While someone created a lattice fence, another couple of kids worked on building a ladder, and yet another devised a pulley system to bring goods up to where we were soon to be stationed. It looked perfect, except that the finished product could only hold a maximum of two at a time. We were not fazed. With the wooden swing on the same tree and the ditch right next to us, we always kept busy while waiting our turn to go up.

As the years passed, the wood rotted and mysterious animal droppings covered the platform. We didn't have the heart to ever tear it down, but we did get creative with new fort construction. When Dad let the field grasses grow tall, my brother and I seized the opportunity to build a top-secret, hidden-in-plain-sight dwelling. First getting the idea from playing hide-and-seek in the tall grasses (alongside the ticks that often entered our house burrowed in the fur of a cat), we started stomping out a circular area like deer bedding down for a nap. Only we weren't getting ready to nap, we were getting ready to create and play! My clever brother devised traps at the entrance by tying together long strands of grass right at foot level. He then created a primitive refrigeration system out of rocks, framing in and covering a small, buried hole in the ground against one "wall" of our fort. The downside of this fort was that if we stood up, we were simply looking down at the crushed grass and were not hidden at all. But it was the perfect place to sit and listen, eat, and be a kid in general.

We spent no money, but we had fun!

- Mom

* * * * *

My oldest brother had coined a nickname for me before he went off to college, and the strange name has stuck to this day. On a warm summer afternoon, our whole family was about to pile in the car to go somewhere, but I simply couldn't wait. I was not normally a hyperactive child, but on this occasion my mom saw the need to wear me out before I was trapped in the car, so she sent me to run a couple laps around the outside of the whole house. I took off running and rounded every corner with as much speed as when I started, and when I promptly returned to the spot where I'd left her, my cheeks were as red as beets. Thus, my brother called me Beets from that day on.

The funny thing is, I am not a mile-a-minute person. I have great regard for an unhurried pace and taking the time to consider and enjoy all things as they come. But this name will forever carry the reminder of the energetic child that is still within me. Every once in a while, it's good to let her out to run around until her cheeks are beet red. And then I realize, there are times to sit and enjoy the breeze gently coming to us, and there are times to get up and create our own gust.

CHAPTER ELEVEN

The iconic lemonade stand is an institution I firmly believe jump-starts many children into being CEOs and heads of marketing campaigns. How else does a person learn the risks of a free market and the worth of a hard-earned dollar (or quarter, as was the case here) than by using charm and wit to coax tenderhearted neighbors and passersby into buying a cup of overly sweetened lemon juice?

For some reason, my siblings and I got the lemonade-stand bug every summer, even though we hardly had through traffic on our street and the speed limit was fifty-five miles per hour—hardly conducive to sudden halts for lemonade. Nonetheless, we always generated income, even if it was seventy-five cents per person at the end of the day (though we never thought about paying our parents back for the ingredients). Occasionally we innovated and added another juice option or a baked good, but the snacks seemed to mysteriously diminish throughout the day as lunchtime got further behind us and our stomachs became more vocal.

Before we called it a day and hauled the leftovers inside (if there were any that survived a bunch of hungry and thirsty kids), we tried one last gimmick to attract customers. Sometimes we scrounged in the garage for colored paper and markers and made the largest signs we could make, and then we waved them madly in the air. Other times we simply used ourselves to draw attention. Our dance routines mainly consisted of poorly executed somersaults and jumping jacks and probably did no good in the advertising sense. But at least they helped us exercise and burn off a little of the sugar we drank from those plastic cups.

* * * * *

There was absolutely nothing that could rival the joy of going camping in the summertime. We were blessed to live only an hour from a picturesque lake nestled in the trees and mountains. It was hidden to the uninformed passerby but burst with delights for those who knew it existed.

As we drove east toward the lake, the sun seemed to burn brighter, the air smelled sweeter, and the tree boughs lining the winding highway waved their arms as if to say, "Welcome to our beautiful abode!" I tingled with excitement as we turned an abrupt right onto a dirt road surrounded by dense forest and then drove into an open area with wetland on either side. The thin road threaded through the swaying grasses and still pools like a single stitch connecting the lake to the highway behind us. As we pushed on through more evergreens (and swarms of mosquitoes in some places), I felt like we'd never stop the car and get out. Finally, as the wheels were still rolling to a stop, I flung the door open and catapulted myself into my dusty, dirty, and perfect second home.

Whether we came for a long day or several nights, only one thing was wrong: our time there was always too short. So much in that place could awaken and inspire all of my senses, not just the beauty I saw with my eyes in every direction. I never got enough of the piney, earthy air in my lungs. The sounds of chipmunks scurrying, woodpeckers beating tree trunks, and waves lapping at the shoreline was the most soothing melody. And while sitting in front of a warm fire, a paper plate of bacon, eggs, and pancakes was a presidential meal.

When we camped with other families from our church, there were endless games to be played: hide-and-seek, kick the can, card games, and putting on light displays in the dark with glow sticks. We caught little frogs, raced to buoys while swimming, and listened to scary stories by firelight. Hearty food (everything tastes better when cooked outdoors), God's creation, and being surrounded by love and acceptance was the formula for a perfect weekend.

Although almost every moment of these lake outings was filled with playing, eating, swimming, or other activities, I had a deep appreciation of my surroundings and often took the time to absorb them. Being away from distractions and free from the fast-paced, daily routine lent itself to a calm that quieted body and soul. As Mom took us on walks to discover varieties of pinecones or find scraps for firewood or watch a glorious, slow-fading sunset, I was deeply aware of God speaking to me through nature. I have never stopped learning priceless lessons by being still, watching, waiting for the voice of God.

> *So beautiful were the trees of deep greens and life-filled colors. The "floor" was carpeted with cushions of ivy that were slipping up to catch the trees, and that glorious sight of complete serenity and oneness of the green land swept my heart away; it almost leaped out of my body. How am I able to describe something beyond all human capacity? My meager attempts do not give justice to what I saw in my Father's land. As I stood in the woods today, silently watching and meditating, he was close-by—ready to give his hand.*

> *- Mom*

*   *   *   *   *

If summer days were characterized by fun and discovery, summer nights represented family bonding and rejuvenation. Whether we gathered to watch a movie in the cozy family room, played card games after a potluck with other families, or enjoyed popcorn and hot chocolate while watching magnificent fireworks on the Fourth of July, there was nowhere else I'd rather be. I thrived in the atmosphere of peace—peace in relationships that was cultivated by love, forgiveness, and grace for each other, and peace in the country, where demands were simpler and the pace was slower.

Even the air was conducive to this, at least on Wednesday nights. As we drove home from midweek church service, looking forward to the hot nachos we traditionally partook of once we got home, we rolled down the car windows as soon as we turned onto our country road. For the next mile, we reveled in "Wednesday night air," which we all agreed was in a class of its own. I'm still not sure what made it so special to us, but I have a guess it was a combination of warm, sweet summer air and the feeling of having just met together with a family of people who loved God and loved each other. There was nothing sweeter.

As I lay in bed at night, tucked in tight with my stuffed animals under my arms and a cat purring at my feet, I opened my ears to the sounds beyond my window. When all was very still, the coyotes felt the urge to begin their howling, sounding somewhat like a bunch of playful puppies romping in an open field under the bright moon and stars. The frogs and crickets cautiously piped up until some intruder or menacing sound made them suddenly stop. Sprinklers systematically covered the thirsty grass with generous showers, singing the most irresistible lullaby: tks, tks, tks, tks, tks, t-t-t-t-t-t, tks, tks, tks, tks, tks, t-t-t-t-t-t. Occasionally a couple raccoons getting into a fight broke the cheerful sounds, but even their high-pitched shrieks were nothing compared to a cougar's eerie scream that sent chills up my spine.

When August lazily rolled around, we eagerly awaited news of meteor showers. Then, if the skies remained clear, we dragged chairs and blankets away from the porch and onto a corner of the lawn, awaiting a spectacular display that rivaled any fireworks show. As we began spotting meteors streaking across the sky, the excitement built and we had contests to determine who could see the most. I once achieved the highly coveted status of "eagle eye" for my high count.

Yes, summer nights were close to perfect. Like a most delectable dessert, they could not be rushed but had to be savored—every last moment.

* * * * *

The warm rays of the sun hitting my arms feel so alive and fresh! Only being outside can do this to me. The birds are busy chattering in the distance, and the swaying gentleness of the tree boughs brings peace to my spirit. How wonderful it is just resting on this stone fence breathing life!

- Mom

I close my eyes and try to imagine the sounds of summer on the two acres I grew up on. Right now there's a war going on; the power of my memory is battling the reality of the snarling highway just past the trees and the nasal-pitched television drifting out a window. Imagination wins. First, silence. I remember when I could hear a single car coming from a half-mile away, and the anticipation of it speeding past our house and down the quiet country road produced a blend of excitement and fear. But between those infrequent installments, blissful quiet reigned.

Something happens when a person gives silence a chance to sing its song. My mom always told me that an hour of boredom leads to an hour of peace. When a person soaks up the quiet, before long many sounds surface and form a harmony unmatched by the most skilled orchestra. Suddenly the trickle of a small ditch becomes as melodic and rhythmic as a rushing river. Bullfrogs pipe up to offer spurts of their long-thought-out commentary. I hear a chipmunk gnawing on a fallen acorn, and the chorus ends with the snap of a twig under the weight of a crouching cat ready to pounce.

It's a world set apart. The cacophony of an overstressed and overcrowded population melts out of my mind and I once again hear the calm of the country. I am swept away.

* * * * *

Why does time fly past before I am able to receive it? Life is short.

- Mom

My days of freedom were numbered. As I sat on "the green box" (a metal electrical box that, though probably unsafe, served a variety of purposes for our play: safe zone for tag, a stand on which to form human statues, and a pommel horse for our field Olympics), I pondered the inevitable change of seasons. Daylight was getting shorter, and before I knew it, I would be attending back-to-school night to learn who my homeroom teacher and classmates would be for another busy school year.

Summer always seemed to have flown by in an instant, and time was a force I was powerless to stop. But new adventures awaited—new friends, added responsibilities, and lots of learning. Rather than resist, I gave in to the current that swept me from summer to fall.

How similar our lives still look as adults. We may not experience cycles of school years and summers of uninhibited play, but we all know seasons and inevitable changes. As my grown-up exterior gets shuffled along in this brief life, my inner child screams at me to never stop being grateful for the simplest of things. The world is confusing, with all its demands and enticing achievements, but the simple beauty of nature stays constant, offering peace and restoration and praising its Creator.

EPILOGUE

How weird are the ties that bind a person to his homeland.

- Mom

Now I sit, years since these precious memories took place, feeling as if I could almost touch my beloved wooden swing or willow tree if I close my eyes. The moment I moved away from that house two years before I graduated from high school, I knew things would never be the same. And sure enough, my path has turned sharp corners, climbed beautiful mountaintops, and dipped into dark, unforeseen valleys since then. But I still carry the love, wonder, and inspiration of my childhood with me through it all. I consider myself immensely blessed to be able to look back on such wonderful years in the country. I owe so much of it to my mom, the resourceful, spunky, devoted woman who held our family together like glue through good times and bad. I know I have a lot of her same personality and outlook, and I try to face challenges and joys with the same attitude she had.

As I put my feet forward for yet another step, I am not held back by wishing for the way things were. Memories must not become strongholds that keep me from advancing in life. Instead, those times I hold dear in my heart propel me forward as I desire to bring not "what was" to the world but "what can be" with the principles I learned early in my life. If we focus our intentions on the most simple, lasting things in life, we will find it easier to create an atmosphere that builds up, heals, and nourishes others. May my journey inspire you to reflect, remodel your motives, if needed, and restore your corner of the world to a more beautiful place.

> *How often do I sit and daydream of living in the country, with beauty still preserved . . .*

- Mom

Made in United States
Troutdale, OR
02/23/2024

17913105R00066